PAWFILE$

PAWFILES

A Bark & smile® Book

By Kim Levin

**Andrews McMeel
Publishing, LLC**

Kansas City

06 07 08 09 10 WKT 10 9 8 7 6 5 4 3 2 1

ISBN-13: 978-0-7407-6066-2
ISBN-10: 0-7407-6066-1

Library of Congress Control Number: 2006922720

www.andrewsmcmeel.com

www.barkandsmile.com

Book design by Holly Camerlinck

Attention: Schools and Businesses
Andrews McMeel books are available at quantity discounts with bulk purchase for educational, business, or sales promotional use. For information, please write to: Special Sales Department, Andrews McMeel Publishing, LLC, 4520 Main Street, Kansas City, Missouri 64111.

For Rachael

Acknowledgments

After publishing several photography gift books, I have often been asked where I find the dogs for my books. The answer is simple. They live in my own backyard. Not literally, but figuratively. For the past eight years, I have traveled the East Coast (and a few other locales throughout the United States) photographing hundreds of dogs. My goal is always the same: to capture the essence, personality, and uniqueness of each dog.

This book is my most personal because it is the first one that features both dog portraits and the personalities behind their portraits. My hope is that it reminds people of their own dogs and what makes them special.

A huge thanks to all of the owners of the dogs that appear in this book. Thanks for taking the time to share your thoughts and stories about your dog. Without you, this book would not be possible.

Thank you to Dorothy O'Brien, my editor and friend, and the terrific team at Andrews McMeel. I am grateful for our continuing partnership over the years, and for your willingness to publish a book that was different from all the rest. Thank you to my black-and-white photo developer Jim Hutchison at Image Makers for your effort, support, and remarkable printing talent. Thank you to El-Co Color Labs for the color prints that appear in *Pawfiles*.

Lastly, thank you to John, Ian, Rachael, and of course, Charlie, my own eccentric and unique dog.

winnie

WINNIE

Age: **Eleven years old**
Breed: **West Highland terrier**
Home: **Monmouth Beach, New Jersey**

Suns herself daily in her strawberry patch and herb garden, smelling regularly of rosemary. Avid squirrel hunter and loyal friend. Personable and endearing. Favorite toys: a duck that squeaks and a frog that ribbits.

THE Amazing MONGRELS

Ages: **All ages**
Breeds: **Rescued mutts**
Home: **On the road**

Smart and sassy. Highly intelligent. Ten-dog troupe travels all over the country, performing to sold-out crowds. Special skills: jumping rope, climbing ladders, walking tightropes, and rolling barrels. Love working the room, the spotlight, and making people smile.

Lilly

LILLY

Age: Ten years old
Breed: Terrier mix
Home: New York, New York

A street dog at heart. Regularly raids the garbage outside her apartment. Chases rats and pigeons in her neighborhood. But don't let her fool you—she has quite expensive taste. Loves filet mignon and crème brûlée.

Anita

ANITA

Age: **Seven years old**
Breed: **Chihuahua mix**
Home: **New York, New York**

Intensely loyal if she likes you. Social butterfly and spoiled rotten. Penchant for high jumping. Eccentric eating habits: separates kibble from bits. Laughs at dogs who play fetch. A real people dog.

CUTTER

Age: **Nine years old**
Breed: **German shepherd**
Home: **Middletown, New Jersey**

Loves animals so much, he visits parks and farms regularly. Favorite farm animals: sheep and horses. He likes your average cat, too. Favorite toy: a dumbbell. It's like his security blanket. Has a backup dumbbell in his home closet. Personable, outgoing, and lovable.

joy

JOY

Age: **Two years old**
Breed: **Dachshund**
Home: **Point Pleasant, New Jersey**

Loves chasing ducks, car rides, playing soccer, and watching golf on TV. Dislikes bathtime and getting her teeth brushed. Burrows under the warm laundry. Sends Christmas cards to all her friends. Knows how to high-five and sing in harmony. Athletic, friendly, and playful.

Lucy

Boomer

LUCY and BOOMER

Ages: Nine years old (Lucy) and eleven years old (Boomer)
Breed: Yellow Labrador retrievers
Home: Colts Neck, New Jersey

They get massages three times a week and give each other daily baths. Lucy is Boomer's biggest cheerleader. Lucy likes talking, belly flops, and running on the treadmill. Boomer likes flirting, being the center of attention, playing catch, and sitting in the driver's seat.

MAX

Age: **Twelve years old**
Breed: **Border collie**
Home: **Previously in New York, New York; now in Elkhart Lake, Wisconsin**

Used to be a city dog, but now enjoys country living. Very bright and persistent. Fluffs his bed until it's comfy and soft. Enjoys the thrill of the hunt, riding shotgun, and butt rubs. Loves ice cubes on hot summer days. Likes chasing squirrels and digging holes. Dislikes suitcases and regular dog biscuits. Thinks he's human.

Owen

O W E N

Age: **One year old**
Breed: **Bull mastiff**
Home: **Red Bank, New Jersey**

Draws his own baths. Consummate snuggler and resident goofball. Loves sleeping with his head on the pillow. Feels no pain. Favorite sport: soccer. Favorite toy: a cow that moos.

PUCK

JAVA, PUCK, and JESSIE

Ages: **Two years old (Java) and four years old (Puck and Jessie)**
Breeds: **Smooth-coated collie (Java), rough collie (Puck), and golden retriever (Jessie)**
Home: **Hardwick, New Jersey**

Java is a goofball and mama's boy. Loves rubbing against feet and herding other dogs. Puck is a handsome gentleman. Refined and loyal, he is the leader of the pack. Jessie is a sock- and dishtowel-hound. Loves kissing, rolling in the grass, and tennis balls. Best of friends.

Earl

E A R L

Age: **Seventeen years old**
Breed: **Jack Russell terrier**
Home: **Middlesex County, New Jersey**

Inspiration for character Earl in the nationally syndicated comic strip *Mutts*. Still looks like a puppy. Great smoocher and sweet soul. In his younger days, Earl was full of life and energy—he literally jumped for joy. Favorite time of day: when the mail (and mailman) arrived. Nowadays, he cries at sad stories, hides his treats, and suns with his cat companion MeeMow. Loves soba noodles, daily walks, and sleeping on his pillow between his mom and dad every night. Nicknames: Early Pearl, Pearl Shnerl, and Shnelly.

Andy

24

ANDY

Age: Ten years old
Breed: Irish setter
Home: Irish Setter Rescue of New Jersey in Whitehouse Station

Laid-back and fun loving. Big goofball. Loves flailing and running around his lake. A real leaner. Enjoys swimming, salads, and soft, squeaky toys. Occasionally lounges on his hammock.

BOSLEY and SAMSON

Ages: **One year old (Bosley) and nine years old (Samson)**
Breeds: **Pug (Bosley) and Akita (Samson)**
Home: **Wappingers Falls, New York**

Samson is a wise old man. Likes empty wrapping paper tubes and sleeping on the office futon. Runs away from home to hang out with the maintenance guys down the street. Bosley is obsessed with Samson. Gives him daily facials and pampers him for hours. Bosley is a neurotic man. Hates the rain. Loves empty water bottles and hanging out in the bathroom.

marlena

MARLENA and AIDAN

Age: **Three years old**
Breed: **Boxers**
Home: **Providence, Rhode Island**

Sister-and-brother dynamic duo. Love making mischief together. Counter surfers extraordinaire. Attached at the hip, they love home-cooked meals, especially meatballs with red sauce and fresh mackerel. Favorite pastimes: running in snowbanks in Vermont, the local dog park, and fighting for position on the couch. Aidan is sweet and anxious. Marlena is calm and patient. Both are sloppy kissers.

BENTLEY

Age: **Seven months old**
Breed: **Newfoundland**
Home: **Middletown, New Jersey**

Thinks he's a lap dog at 125 pounds. Loves to ride in the tractor and visit the cows on his farm.
Best friend: an African gray parrot named Rudy. Sleeps in the shower stall. Loves peanut butter–filled
Kongs. People pleaser.

JACK

Age: Five years old
Breed: Labrador mix
Home: Cape Cod, Massachusetts

Sweet and loyal. Loves road trips, clambakes, and the surf. A dog's dog. Favorite breed: Yorkies, Westies, Jack Russells. Guess he's a terrier guy. Hates traffic and rainstorms.

Oliver

A U R I and O L I V E R

Ages: **Four years old (Auri) and two years old (Oliver)**
Breeds: **German shepherd (Auri) and English bulldog (Oliver)**
Home: **Oceanport, New Jersey**

A gentle soul, Auri thinks she is Oliver's mother. Loves to groom and bathe him. Used to love TV but now barks incessantly at everything on it. Oliver is a digger and a nondiscriminating eater. Obsessed with Beanie Babies and his bed. Also known as Truck Driver.

Codi

Hugo

CODI and HUGO

Ages: Eleven years old (Codi) and two years old (Hugo)
Breeds: English bulldog (Codi) and French bulldog (Hugo)
Home: Montclair, New Jersey

One word: sibling rivalry. Codi is a loving spirit. Snores loudly. A great hostess. Favorite spot: sunning herself on the den couch. Smiles even with her underbite. Hugo is Mr. Romantic. Cries at sappy movies. Hates it when he doesn't get his way. Favorite toy: stuffed elephant named Nummy.

Bumpus

BUMPUS

Age: **Eight years old**
Breed: **Border collie**
Home: **Oceanport, New Jersey**

Being blind hasn't stopped him from operating at two speeds: zero and overdrive. Couch potato by day and high jumper by night. Favorite spot: his rocking chair where he reads the daily paper. Loves prancing, dancing, and Greenies.

Charlie

CHARLIE

Age: **Seven years old**
Breed: **Border collie/greyhound mix**
Home: **Little Silver, New Jersey**

Eccentric and unique. An extremely picky eater. Cassanova kisser. Special skills: singing to the harmonica, piano, and Irish bagpipes. Petrified of fireworks, thunder, and cell phones. Consummate digger and ruiner of comforters. Loves stuffed animals, stalking rabbits, peanut butter, and tummy rubs. Barks for treats.

otis

wiley

WILEY and OTIS

Ages: Eleven years old (Wiley) and five years old (Otis)
Breeds: White German shepherd mix (Wiley) and wire fox terrier (Otis)
Home: Tinton Falls, New Jersey

It's a love-hate relationship. Otis adores Wiley and Wiley tolerates Otis. Wiley loves riding in the car with her head out the window. Loves carrots, beef, and chasing deer. Otis is a comedian. Takes swimming lessons and Rollerblades. Has yearly birthday parties and goes to doggy day care. Boings regularly.

Ragan

R A G A N

Age: **Three months old**
Breed: **Jack Russell terrier**
Home: **Previously in New York City; now in Seattle, Washington**

A hugger and digger. Loves to run in circles and tug at her chew toys. Suffers from acute separation anxiety. Misses the big city but is getting used to the Seattle rain. Frisky and friendly.

FLOYD

Age: Two years old
Breed: Bassett hound
Home: Mamaroneck, New York

A love hound. Submissive and needy, he whines for attention. Early riser yet sleeps all day. Loves sleeping on the ottoman and bed. A true people dog. Nickname: the Mayor of Mamaroneck.

jewlsie

JEWLSIE

Age: **Three years old**
Breed: **Red border collie**
Home: **Freehold, New Jersey**

A girly girl. Loves to shop at Petco and PetSmart. Doesn't like the rain. Trots like a pony. Prissy, intuitive, and playful. Pokes and butt checks. Favorite toy: Hurl-A-Squirrel.

Hunter

H U N T E R

Age: **Seven years old**
Breed: **German shorthaired pointer**
Home: **Middletown, New Jersey**

A true gentleman. Recently married his sweetheart, Bailey. In love with his hammock. Constantly searching for missing tennis balls. Loves the outdoors, belly rubs, and hugs. Patient, loyal, and funny.

JOY

Age: **Eight years old**
Breed: **Siberian husky**
Home: **Delray Beach, Florida**

Singing sensation. Has a song for her every mood. Runs in circles every night to get comfortable. Bed hog. Loves sleeping all day, snuggling, and swimming. Warm, independent, and talkative.

TUCK

T U C K

Age: **Three months old**
Breed: **Rhodesian ridgeback**
Home: **Little Silver, New Jersey**

Mischievous troublemaker. Steals baby's food and toys. Has a special fondness for plastic farm animals. A lover and a 'fraidy cat.

TINA

Age: Six years old
Breed: Black Labrador/pit bull mix
Home: Brooklyn, New York

Quirky, bright, and outgoing. A true Gemini: moody and sweet. Dramatic actress. Loves cheeseburgers, sunbathing, and poking. Dislikes baths, rainstorms, and getting wet. Also known as Queena.

LULUBELLE

Age: Nine years old
Breed: Bassett hound
Home: Oceanport, New Jersey

Doesn't laugh often, but she thinks she's a riot. Loves carrots, tomatoes, and chasing her cat Mikayla. Hates manicures and her cat Iris. Sits for cookies—all three feet and ninety pounds of her.

Princess   Melody

PRINCESS, MELODY, and MADISON

Ages: Seven years old (Princess and Melody) and ten years old (Madison)
Breeds: Terrier mix (Princess) and Jack Russell terriers (Melody and Madison)
Home: Allentown, New Jersey

Princess was rescued from Grand Cayman Islands. Loves being the center of attention and has a penchant for squeaky toys. Melody communicates by giving kisses with a growl and her teeth showing. Will do anything for a dip in the pool. Madison is highly intelligent. Caregiver and therapist. Carries her toys to the car (along with the keys) after shopping at PetSmart.

JOSIE

Age: **Three years old**
Breed: **Labrador mix**
Home: **South Plainfield, New Jersey**

Sunbathes on both sides. Loves Frisbee, burying bones, crunchy vegetables, and birdseed. At Christmas, she ate a pound of peppermint patties, including the wrappers. Enjoys agility, hiking, and her pet sitter, Miss Susan.

MUGGINS

Age: **Four years old**
Breed: **English bulldog**
Home: **Morris Plains, New Jersey**

Takes daily walks to the corner store for free cannoli and BBQ squirrels. Last year he dressed as Muggins Maximus for Halloween. Needs to be woken up in the morning. Couch stealer. Special skill: balances on hind legs. Favorite thing to do: suckle his pet monkey. Nickname: Sweetpeach.

Muggins

johnnie walker

JOHNNIE WALKER

Age: Eleven years old
Breed: Scottish terrier
Home: Long Branch, New Jersey

Refined and elegant. Singleminded approach to life. Expert in training his mom and dad to obey. Loves to patrol street from his seventh-floor balcony. Enjoys playing catch, dissecting squeaky toys, and having his back and ears scratched. Adores apples and watermelon and sniffing each blade of grass on his daily walk.

SUSIE and THOR

Ages: Seven years old (Susie) and four years old (Thor)
Breed: German shepherds
Home: White Bear Lake, Minnesota

Mother and son. In their heydey, Susie and Thor worked as therapy dogs with Parkinson's patients. Susie is the grand dame of the house. Doesn't bark or fuss to get her way—simply nudges with her nose and stares. Refined and patient. Thor is a sweet and snuggly big baby. Favorite game: hide and seek. Has a huge toy box filled to the brim with squeakies and plushies. Outside, he's a wild man— loves to run figure eights and chase his mommy.

SALTY

Age: **Five months old**
Breed: **Shetland sheepdog**
Home: **Brick, New Jersey**

An old curmudgeon. Loves to bark and bully his four cats. Passionate about any toy he can sink his teeth into. Tends to shake all over from sheer excitement when kids are around. Nickname: Napoleon.

sandy

SANDY

Age: Five years old
Breed: German shepherd/Basenji mix
Home: Harrisonburg, Virginia

Rescued at six months. Enjoys swimming in the Delaware Canal and chasing waves. Runs 5K races. Favorite food: pork spare ribs. Likes large men with facial hair. Dislikes all vegetables. Has extreme phobia of cell phones and thunderstorms. Loves life.

Gryffindor

GRYFFINDOR

Age: **Two years old**
Breed: **Pug/terrier mix**
Home: **Little Silver, New Jersey**

Jealous lover. Protective and loyal. A one-woman dog even though he lives with four (as well as one cat and four parrots). Likes car rides, running in circles, carrots, and green beans. Nickname: Commander-in-chief.

KYLIE

Age: **Four months old**
Breed: **Irish setter**
Home: **Boston, Massachusetts**

Sweet, independent, and extremely hyper. Has a fondness for barking at nothing and destroying household items such as flip-flops, eyeglasses, and leather furniture. Loves going off-leash at the dog park. Plays submissively with her park buddy, Hey Hey the beagle. Enjoys stalking pigeons, learning how to swim, and doggy day care. When she runs in the sunlight, she's breathtaking.

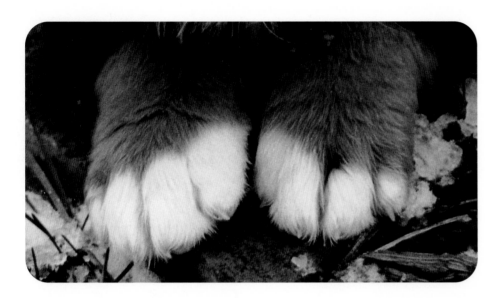

Ben

BEN

Age: **Four months old**
Breed: **Bernese mountain dog**
Home: **Middletown, New Jersey**

Laid-back slacker. Favorite game: tail tug-of-war. Insists water be served in the toilet. Has an awesome sense of interior design—leaves his fur in every corner of the house. Loves napping, lounging, and taking it easy. Ben is now a 125-pound lap dog.

SAMMY

Age: **Six years old**
Breed: **Pit bull**
Home: **Old Bridge, New Jersey**

Spends her days sleeping on the couch and following patches of sunlight in the window.
Couch potato by day and loyal protector by night. Frolics at the beach in the summer. Gentle, sweet, and happy. Gives sloppy kisses. Favorite food: pizza.

Ghost and Rocky

GHOST and ROCKY

Age: **Five years old**
Breeds: **Yellow Labrador mix (Ghost) and bunny (Rocky)**
Home: **Middletown, New Jersey**

Ghost is silly and happy-go-lucky. Loves to chase squirrels and hang with Rocky. Afraid of thunderstorms. Nickname: Gong Gong. Translation in Taiwanese: silly and not so smart. Rocky has a little kick in her step. She loves running and jumping. Friendly and mellow. Named after Rocky Balboa because of her black eyes.

sparkie

SPARKIE

Age: **Seven years old**
Breed: **Shih tzu**
Home: **New York, New York**

Watches the neighborhood cats from her apartment window. Has a penchant for old shoulder pads and socks. Rips the squeakies out of her toys. Loves the day spa, sleeping nose to nose, and daily walks in Central Park. Hides in the bathtub during storms. Waves paws when excited.

SPECK and SPIKE

Ages: **Ten years old (Speck) and nine years old (Spike)**
Breed: **Chihuahuas**
Home: **Montclair, New Jersey**

Speck, aka Girly, is friendly and happy. Likes chasing squirrels, deer, and even airplanes. Kind to strangers. Crazy about having her back scratched. Favorite food: everything except lettuce. Spike, aka Boyzo, is wimpy and manipulative. Barks at everything and everyone. Favorite toy: his green blanket named Stinky Green.

Max

M A X

Age: **One year old**
Breed: **Black standard poodle**
Home: **Morristown, New Jersey**

Well educated, intelligent, and an independent thinker. Attended boarding school with the Monks of New Skete. Spends his days working as a therapy dog. Wags his tail and greets patients with his paw. Maintains a busy social schedule: playdates at the dog park and seeing movies at the drive-in. Loves rawhide, popcorn, and tummy rubs.

OZZIE and WILBUR

Age: **Three years old**
Breeds: **Striped tabby (Ozzie) and Dachshund (Wilbur)**
Home: **New York, New York**

Ozzie loves watching birds on TV, eating Wilbur's food, and poking holes in comforters. Hates eating his own food and tall dogs. Wilbur loves destroying toys and napping with Ozzie. Also admires his oblong shape. Extremely agoraphopic. Dislikes toys that can't be destroyed, leaving his apartment, and the daily grind.

wally

W A L L Y

Age: **Ten years old**
Breed: **Pug**
Home: **New York, New York**

Real name: Walrus. Nicknames: too many to list. Has a staff of two pug assistants, caretakers on the Upper East Side, and a vet that makes house calls. Spends her days sleeping on the daybed, leather ottoman, and velvet sofa. Spends her evenings anticipating her dinner and arranging her pillows for maximum comfort. Favorite things to do: taking a "mosey," sleeping with overnight guests, dinner parties, and barking at toll booths.

Tino

Tara

TINO and TARA

Ages: **One year old (Tino) and twelve years old (Tara)**
Breeds: **Spinone Italiano (Tino) and Bracco Italiano (Tara)**
Home: **Spinone Italiano Rescue in Whitehouse Station, New Jersey**

Tino is short for *Bello Tino Piccolo Uno.* Italian translation: handsome Tino. Loves to swim, hang out, and cuddle with kids. Docile, strong, and friendly. Tara's official name is Tiramisu. Loves to hunt and play by herself. Loyal, gentle, and intelligent. Uses her doelike eyes to get what she wants.

TRUMAN and DARLA

Age: **Three years old**
Breed: **Bernese mountain dogs**
Home: **Long Branch, New Jersey**

Brother and sister, they are polar opposites. Truman is
independent and a bit of a loner. Loves baths, sunning on the
patio, and athletics. Darla is personable and friendly. Loves to
eat, sleep in the shade, and lead Truman on daily adventures.

K I R A

Age: **Five years old**
Breed: **Chow chow**
Home: **New York, New York**

Lives with feline sisters, Tara and Rosie. Loves to chase them and steal their toys. Aloof with strangers, but friendly to every dog she meets on the street. Flirtatious. Gentle, tolerant, and patient. Dislikes getting wet. Must have umbrella in the rain. Favorite spot: the bagel shop at the corner of York Avenue and 76th Street.

Simon

S I M O N

Age: **Six years old**
Breed: **Golden retriever**
Home: **Minneapolis, Minnesota**

Free spirit. Graceful and funny. Special talent: vocalizations and singing. Has a distinct bark for all occasions: "alarm" bark, "you're home" bark, and "throw the ball" bark. Greatest achievement: his very own CD. Loves sitting by your side. Passion for people, tennis balls, and water.

whitesox

WHITESOX

Age: Thirteen years old
Breed: German shepherd mix
Home: Hazlet, New Jersey

Fiercely loyal. Loves chasing watermelons in the pool. Enjoys going to work and eating anything with peanut butter. Dislikes manicures and dressing in Halloween costumes. Named after his family's favorite baseball team.

Rocky

ROCKY

Age: **Three months old**
Breed: **Norwich terrier**
Home: **Rumson, New Jersey**

High-spirited and fearless. Troublemaker. Enjoys sleeping late every morning and meeting his friends for afternoon walks in the woods. Kisses anyone who is willing.

MACKENZIE

Age: **Three months old**
Breed: **West Highland terrier**
Home: **Red Bank, New Jersey**

Rings the bell to go outside. Lays on windowsill and talks to her dog neighbors. Loves jumping through handmade hoops, chewing sofa corners, and running in circles. Passionate kisser, hugger, and couch potato.

sweetpea

SWEETPEA

Age: **Eighteen years old**
Breed: **Chihuahua**
Home: **Atlantic Highlands, New Jersey**

Feisty despite being blind and deaf. Energizer bunny. Favorite spot: a purple mushy bed with her security blanket. Needs dental work.

J. R.

Age: Six years old
Breed: Jack Russell terrier
Home: Atlantic Highlands, New Jersey

Has to be on the go: driving, swimming, running. Always looking for critters to chase. A true yoga dog: flexible, trusting, and independent. Bed hog by night. Cuddler by day. Saves kisses for special occasions.

Otto

O T T O

Age: Two years old
Breed: Golden retriever/beagle mix
Home: Verona, New Jersey

The only beagle part of Otto is the white tip on his tail and his howl. Likes climbing his fort and going down the slide. Favorite game: chasing squirrels and rabbits but has never been fast enough to catch one. Loves kids.

George

G E O R G E

Age: **Twelve years old**
Breed: **Corgi/terrier mix**
Home: **Chicago, Illinois**

Big flirt. Easygoing and laid-back. Smiles when he sleeps. Has a fondness for Spanish radio and music. Loves daily walks and greeting his neighbors. Fear of bicycles and rakes. Favorite food: burritos.

ABBY and ZOE

Ages: **Eleven years old (Abby) and two years old (Zoe)**
Breeds: **Yellow Labrador (Abby) and labradoodle (Zoe)**
Home: **Warren, New Jersey**

Zoe and Abby are sugar and spice. Zoe is sweet and reserved. She loves to watch the world go by. Loves people, yogurt, and belly rubs. Abby is spunky and quirky. Intelligent and mischievous. Has boundless energy. She loves to run around the yard and take flying leaps. Loves sports, riding in the car, and having things her way.

JAKE

Age: **Five years old**
Breed: **Pit bull mix**
Home: **Tinton Falls, New Jersey**

Loyal confidant and friend. Loves long walks on the beach, stick chewing, and family celebrations. Demands a pig's ear when he's been a good boy. He even knows where they're hidden in the closet. Enjoys snuggling by the fireplace in the winter and sunning himself on the porch in the summer.

spike

SPIKE

Age: **Four years old**
Breed: **English bulldog**
Home: **Little Silver, New Jersey**

Lives a wonderful life even with chronic hip pain. Lover and protector. Likes bathing in the kitchen sink, eating bubbles, and sneaking naps on the leather sofa. Snores loud and farts even louder. Thinks he's a lap dog. Instinctively knows when you're sad. Has occasional wanderlust.

J. D.

Age: **Seven years old**
Breed: **Beagle/terrier mix**
Home: **Wall, New Jersey**

Velcro dog. Attached to your hip. Pet therapist and volunteer ambassador. Social butterfly and dresses up for parties. Loves to bow, roll, and spoon. Does not fetch on command.

SIMONE

Age: **Seven years old**
Breed: **Standard poodle**
Home: **Little Silver, New Jersey**

Airhead by day and tramp by night. Feminine and flighty. Loves to sing with her parrots, Roscoe, Floyd, and Gato. Great watchdog. Gives fabulous hugs.

SHORTY

Age: **Eight years old**
Breed: **Bassett hound**
Home: **Little Silver, New Jersey**

Extremely stubborn and gregarious. Loves to gab. Likes playing with her siblings, even though they don't reciprocate her feelings. Slowly realizing life would be easier as an only dog. Adores kissing, Milk-Bones, and chatting on the phone.

NAOMI

Age: **Four years old**
Breed: **Afghan hound**
Home: **Long Branch, New Jersey**

Beauty queen. Refined, sweet, and timid. Loves to cuddle stuffed animals and people. Runs with grace and style. Strict vegetarian. Loves carrots, squash, and broccoli.

In memory of Lilly, Puck, Codi, Johnnie Walker,
Thor, Sweetpea, Jewlsie, Simon, and Whitesox